First World War
and Army of Occupation
War Diary
France, Belgium and Germany

21 DIVISION
Divisional Troops
Divisional Ammunition Column
12 September 1915 - 30 April 1919

WO95/2143/4

The Naval & Military Press Ltd
www.nmarchive.com
Published in association with The National Archives

Published by

The Naval & Military Press Ltd

Unit 10 Ridgewood Industrial Park,

Uckfield, East Sussex,

TN22 5QE England

Tel: +44 (0) 1825 749494

www.naval-military-press.com

www.nmarchive.com

This diary has been reprinted in facsimile from the original. Any imperfections are inevitably reproduced and the quality may fall short of modern type and cartographic standards.

© Crown Copyright
Images reproduced by permission of The National Archives, London, England, 2015.

Contents

Document type	Place/Title	Date From	Date To
Heading	2143/4 Divisional Ammunition Column.		
Heading	21st Division Divl Ammn Column Sep 1915-Apr 1919		
Heading	21st Division 21st Div L. Ammunition Column Vol I Sep 1 15		
War Diary	Havre	12/09/1915	13/09/1915
War Diary	Audruicq	14/09/1915	15/09/1915
War Diary	Zouafques	16/09/1915	20/09/1915
War Diary	Arques	21/09/1915	21/09/1915
War Diary	Lambres	22/09/1915	22/09/1915
War Diary	Lieres	23/09/1915	23/09/1915
War Diary	Bruay	24/09/1915	24/09/1915
War Diary	Noeux Les Mines	24/09/1915	30/09/1915
Miscellaneous	Appendix I. Composition of Transports		
Heading	21st Division 21st Divl. A.C. Vol 2 Oct 15		
War Diary	Noeux Les Mines	04/10/1915	04/10/1915
War Diary	Regnier	05/10/1915	05/10/1915
War Diary	Hondeghem	24/10/1915	25/10/1915
War Diary	St. Jans Cappel	27/10/1915	27/10/1915
Heading	21st D.A.C. Vol 3, 4 Nov 15 Dec 15		
War Diary	St Jans Cappel	30/11/1915	05/12/1915
Heading	21st Divisional Artillery. 21st Divisional Ammunition Column R.F.A. January 1916		
War Diary	St Jan Cappel	31/01/1916	31/01/1916
Heading	21st Divisional Artillery. 21st Divisional Ammunition Column R.F.A. February 1916		
War Diary	St Jan Cappel	29/02/1916	29/02/1916
Heading	21st Divisional Artillery. 21st Divisional Ammunition Column R.F.A. March 1916		
War Diary	Nieppe	24/03/1916	24/03/1916
War Diary	La Creche	26/03/1916	26/03/1916
Heading	21st Divisional Artillery 21st Divisional Ammunition Column R.F.A. April 1916		
War Diary	St Jan Cappel	01/04/1916	01/04/1916
War Diary	Borre	02/04/1916	02/04/1916
War Diary	St Jan Cappel	02/04/1916	02/04/1916
War Diary	Bussey les Daours	10/04/1916	12/04/1916
Heading	21st Divisional Artillery. 21st Divisional Ammunition Column R.F.A. May 1916		
War Diary	Buire	11/05/1916	23/05/1916
Miscellaneous	Adjutant Generals Office Base	02/06/1916	02/06/1916
Heading	21st Divisional Artillery War Diary Missing 21st Divisional Ammunition Column R.F.A. June 1916		
Heading	21st Divisional Artillery. 21st Divisional Ammunition Column R.F.A. July 1916		
War Diary	Buire	01/07/1916	01/07/1916
War Diary	Meaulte	08/07/1916	20/07/1916
War Diary	Fricourt	23/07/1916	23/07/1916
War Diary	Vivier Mill	25/07/1916	25/07/1916
War Diary	Argoeuves	26/07/1916	26/07/1916
War Diary	Bourdon	27/07/1916	27/07/1916

War Diary	St Riquier	29/07/1916	29/07/1916
War Diary	Wavans	30/07/1916	30/07/1916
Miscellaneous	Headquarters, 21st Divisional Artillery	01/08/1916	01/08/1916
Heading	21st Divisional Artillery, 21st Divisional Ammunition Column R.F.A. August 1916		
War Diary	Berlancourt	03/08/1916	28/08/1916
Miscellaneous	Situation 13 8 16 125 Bde RFA		
Heading	21st Divisional Artillery. 21st Divisional Ammunition Column R.F.A. September 1916		
War Diary	Montenes Court	08/09/1916	08/09/1916
War Diary	Wamin	10/09/1916	10/09/1916
War Diary	Rozieres	12/09/1916	12/09/1916
War Diary	Vauchelles	13/09/1916	13/09/1916
War Diary	Albert	13/09/1916	13/09/1916
War Diary	Mametz	14/09/1916	15/09/1916
Heading	21st Divisional Artillery. 21st Divisional Ammunition Column R.F.A. October 1916		
War Diary	Mametz	02/10/1916	15/10/1916
War Diary	La Neuville	16/10/1916	16/10/1916
War Diary	Talmas	17/10/1916	17/10/1916
War Diary	Orville	18/10/1916	18/10/1916
War Diary	Ligny-Sur Canche	19/10/1916	19/10/1916
War Diary	Anvin	20/10/1916	20/10/1916
War Diary	Labouvriere	22/10/1916	22/10/1916
Heading	21st Divisional Artillery 21st Divisional Ammunition Colum R.F.A. November 1916		
Heading	21st Divisional Ammunition Column Vol 15		
Heading	21st Divisional Artillery. 21st Divisional Ammunition Column R.F.A. December 1916		
War Diary	Verquigneul	01/12/1916	05/01/1917
War Diary	Annezin	14/01/1917	28/01/1917
War Diary	Caudescure	29/01/1917	29/01/1917
War Diary	Herzeele	12/02/1917	12/02/1917
War Diary	Hazebrouck	13/02/1917	13/02/1917
War Diary	Rien-Du Vinage	16/02/1917	16/02/1917
War Diary	Verquigneul	05/03/1917	05/03/1917
War Diary	Rien-Du-Vinage	11/03/1917	11/03/1917
War Diary	Heuchin	13/03/1917	13/03/1917
War Diary	Aubrometz	14/03/1917	14/03/1917
War Diary	Barly	15/03/1917	15/03/1917
War Diary	Lucheux	16/03/1917	16/03/1917
War Diary	Guoy-En-Artois	23/03/1917	23/03/1917
War Diary	Monchiet	24/03/1917	31/03/1917
War Diary	Boyelles	16/05/1917	16/05/1917
War Diary	Bailleul Mont	09/04/1917	11/04/1917
War Diary	Boiry St. Rictrude	12/04/1917	12/04/1917
War Diary	Rictrude	20/04/1917	23/04/1917
War Diary	Boiry St. Rictrude	22/06/1917	10/07/1917
War Diary	Boiry Becquerelle	22/08/1917	22/08/1917
War Diary	Boiry St. Rictrude	05/09/1917	05/09/1917
War Diary	Hopoutre Godewaers Svelde Caistre	06/09/1917	14/09/1917
War Diary	Reninghelst Area	14/09/1917	30/09/1917
War Diary	Zevecoten	20/10/1917	20/10/1917
War Diary	Cafe Belge	14/11/1917	14/11/1917
War Diary	Reninghelst	15/11/1917	15/11/1917
War Diary	Morbecque	17/11/1917	17/11/1917

War Diary	Annezin	18/11/1917	18/11/1917
War Diary	Ourton	19/11/1917	19/11/1917
War Diary	Olhain	21/11/1917	21/11/1917
War Diary	Anzin St Aubin	29/11/1917	29/11/1917
War Diary	Anzin	01/12/1917	01/12/1917
War Diary	Beaulincourt	02/12/1917	04/12/1917
War Diary	Longavesnes	08/12/1917	08/12/1917
War Diary	Tincourt Wood	21/01/1918	21/01/1918
War Diary	Driencourt	12/02/1918	23/03/1918
War Diary	Bray Sur Somme	25/03/1918	25/03/1918
War Diary	Contay	28/03/1918	28/03/1918
Heading	21st Divisional Artillery. 21st Divisional Ammunition Column R.F.A. April 1918		
War Diary	Behencourt	28/03/1918	06/04/1918
War Diary	Querrieu	06/04/1918	12/04/1918
War Diary	Hem	12/04/1918	14/04/1918
War Diary	Abeele	14/04/1918	18/04/1918
War Diary	Eecke	18/04/1918	03/05/1918
War Diary	S Momelin	04/05/1918	04/05/1918
War Diary	S. Omer Arques Wizernes	05/05/1918	06/05/1918
War Diary	Bouleuse	06/05/1918	06/05/1918
War Diary	Savigny	07/05/1918	07/05/1918
War Diary	Aougny	07/05/1918	14/05/1918
War Diary	Chateau Au Boy De Large	14/05/1918	27/05/1918
War Diary	Vandeuil	27/05/1918	28/05/1918
War Diary	Ste C	28/05/1918	29/05/1918
War Diary	Laneuville	29/05/1918	29/05/1918
War Diary	Sdenus	30/05/1918	30/05/1918
War Diary	Damery	12/06/1918	15/06/1918
War Diary	Vaux Pre	16/06/1918	21/06/1918
War Diary	Bouttencourt	22/06/1918	22/06/1918
War Diary	St Martin Le Gaillard Area	30/06/1918	30/06/1918
War Diary	Bouttencourt	21/07/1918	23/07/1918
War Diary	Lealvilliers	24/07/1918	24/07/1918
War Diary	Mailly Maillet	24/07/1918	24/07/1918
War Diary	Beaucourt Sur Ancre	25/07/1918	26/07/1918
War Diary	P V S	03/08/1918	03/08/1918
War Diary	Le Sars	07/09/1918	07/09/1918
War Diary	Manancourt Area	09/09/1918	30/09/1918
War Diary	Elsom Copse	30/09/1918	30/09/1918
Heading	War Diary 21st Divisional Ammunition Column. October 1st-31st 1918		
War Diary	Elsom Copse	07/10/1918	07/10/1918
War Diary	Gengwell Copse	08/10/1918	08/10/1918
War Diary	M 33	11/10/1918	11/10/1918
War Diary	J 31 a 6.5	23/10/1918	23/10/1918
Heading	War Diary Of 21st Divisional Ammunition Column R.F.A. From 1st November 1918 To 30th November 1918		
War Diary	Amerval	04/11/1918	05/11/1918
War Diary	Poix Du Nord	07/11/1918	07/11/1918
War Diary	Lucquinel	10/11/1918	10/11/1918
War Diary	Avmieres	11/11/1918	15/11/1918
Heading	War Diary Of 21st Divisional Ammunition Column R.F.A. From December 1st. To December 31st 1918		
War Diary	Montay	11/12/1918	13/12/1918

War Diary	Ailbenchiel Aux Bois	14/12/1918	14/12/1918
War Diary	Buire	15/12/1918	15/12/1918
War Diary	Chuignoles	16/12/1918	16/12/1918
War Diary	Boutillerie	17/12/1918	17/12/1918
War Diary	St. Bauveur	01/01/1919	31/01/1919
Heading	War Diary Of 21st Divisional Ammunition Column, R.F.A. From 1st February 1919 To 28th February 1919		
War Diary	St. Sauveur	01/02/1919	30/04/1919

2143/4

Divisional Ammunition Column.

21ST DIVISION

DIVL AMMN COLUMN
SEP 1915 – APR 1919

121/6930

21st Division

Int: Sit L: Ammunition Column
vol I
Sept. 15

apr 19

WAR DIARY
or
INTELLIGENCE SUMMARY.
(Erase heading not required.)

Army Form C. 2118

Place	Date	Hour	Summary of Events and Information	Remarks and references to Appendices
(Above) HAVRE	1915 12 Sept	10.30 a.m.	**21st Divisional Ammunition Column** The unit arrived at Le Havre, in 3 transports the composition of which is shown as an appendix.	App. I. W.E.
(Above) HAVRE	13 Sept	7.30 a.m.	The unit comprising has now entrained — strewn in all — number across rows. The composition of each train is shown as an Appendix	App II. W.E.
Audruicq	14 Sept	2 p.m.	Headquarters + ⅓ of No 1 Section arrived by train + proceeded to Billets at WOLPHUS. — Sections are billeted at ZOUAFQUES.	W.E.
AUDRUICQ	15 Sept	9 a.m.	Information received that Ammunition as follows was available for issue from 21st Ammunition Sub Park + refilling D.A.C. coved commenced at 3.45 p.m. to day at Cross roads N.E. of O. in LA RECOUSSE. (Sheet 5A. Order Map. 1:100,000. HAZEBROUCK.) Ammunition 18 Pdr H.E. — 75 sq Rd. — 2 W.E. 18 Pdr (S). — 3954 2" W.E. 4.5 How. H.E. — 720.	W.E.

Army Form C. 2118

WAR DIARY
or
INTELLIGENCE SUMMARY.
(Erase heading not required.)

West ?

Instructions regarding War Diaries and Intelligence Summaries are contained in F.S. Regs., Part II and the Staff Manual respectively. Title pages will be prepared in manuscript.

Place	Date	Hour	Summary of Events and Information	Remarks and references to Appendices
ZOUAFQUES	16-9-15	3.30 p.m.	21st Divisional Ammn Column. The following rounds of Gun Ammunition were received from Railhead.	WF
			Sub-Park	
			18 Pdr Shrap. 1352	
ZOUAFQUES	19-9-15	9 p.m.	Movement. Orders received from HQ RA to hold unit in readiness to move by march route to LA RECOUSSE - time 8 p.m. on the matter. Starting point arranged N of LA Vn LA RECOUSSE (Sheet 5A HAZEBROUCK)	WF
— —	20-9-15	8 p.m.	Left ZOUAFQUES & proceeded by march route to ARQUES, ordered into bivouac at FORT ROUGE.	WF
ARQUES	21-9-15		Left ARQUES Moved by march route to LAMBRES where unit went into bivouac.	WF

Army Form C. 2118
Sheet No 3

WAR DIARY
or
INTELLIGENCE SUMMARY.
(Erase heading not required.)

Instructions regarding War Diaries and Intelligence Summaries are contained in F. S. Regs., Part II. and the Staff Manual respectively. Title pages will be prepared in manuscript.

Place	Date	Hour	Summary of Events and Information	Remarks and references to Appendices
LAMBRES	29/9/15	8 pm	The test preceded by mounted scouts to LIERES, + were met by Russets.	JBF
LIERES	23/9/15	9 am	Ammunition Orders received to exchange 152 rounds per Brigade Ammn Column (9th - 95th + 96th) 7 M. Plr charged for 18 Pdr. High Explosive. The service was completed by 12-15 pm to day.	JBF JBF
BRUAY	24/9/15	6 am	Arrived from LIERES, left at 2.30 pm + NOEUX les MINES, where we arrived at 6-30 pm Division in action. An advanced Section was established at Crossroads L.11.a. Centred map BETHUNE. This section is reports from Hd. Qs. + supplies all B/de Ammn Columns of the Division	JBF JBF JBF
NOEUX les MINES	24/9/15 to 30/9/15			

J B Henderson Major RHA
Army 21st Div. Ammn Col.

Appendix 1.

Composition of Transports

No. 2 Section   "H.T. Blackwell"

No. 3 Section   "H.T. Anglo Canadian"

No. 1 Section & Head Quarters   "H.T. African Prince"

Appendix II

Composition of Trains

Station of Entrainment. Gare de Marchandises Havre.
  "   " Detrainment. "Audruicq".

1st Train.	2/3	of No 1 Section
2nd "	2/3	of No 2 Section
3rd "	2/3	of No 3 Section
4th "	1/3	of No 2 Section
	1/3	of No 3 Section
5th "	1/3	of No 1 Section
		+ Headquarters

121/7430

21st Hussars

Jor. Sirk: A.C.
& #2

Oct 15

WAR DIARY
or
INTELLIGENCE SUMMARY. 21st Divisional Ammn Column

Army Form C. 2118.

First Sheet

(Erase heading not required.)

Place	Date	Hour	Summary of Events and Information	Remarks and references to Appendices
Noeux les Mines	4/10/15	6 am	The Column proceeded by march route to MERVILLE via SAILLY-LABOURSE and BETHUNE – Billeted for the night at REGNIER.	AWG
REGNIER	5/10/15	10 am	Column continued the march and arrived at HONDEGHEM via HAZEBROUCK. Headquarters billeted at a farm. V.13.a, No 1 Section at U.6.(a).7.6. No 2 Section at O.30.(c).9. – No 3 Section at V.13.(d) Reference SHEET 27 BELGIUM + FRANCE.	AWG
HONDEGHEM	24/10/15	6-30 am	No 3 Section proceeded by march route to NIEPPE + relieved advanced Section of 50th Divl. Ammn. Coln.	AWG
HONDEGHEM	25/10/15	9 am	Head Quarters + No 1 + 2 Sections proceeded by march route to ST JANS CAPPEL in relay of 50th Divl. Ammn Column.	AWG
ST JANS CAPPEL	27/10/15	11-30 am	H.M. the KING inspected 21st DIVISION at BAILLEUL. Lt. R.G. BELL and 4 NCO's + men attended from 21st DIVL AMMN COLN	AWG

J.D. Anderson Lt RFA
Commanding 21st Divl Amm Coln

2nd copy.
vols 3, 4

1928
15

Nov '15
Dec '15

WAR DIARY
or
INTELLIGENCE SUMMARY.

(Erase heading not required.)

Army Form C. 2118

21st DIV. A.M.N. COL.   Nov't

Place	Date	Hour	Summary of Events and Information	Remarks and references to Appendices
G Jais Cappe.	30/11/,915.		There is nothing of note to record. The unit occupied billets as in previous month. There are no casualties.	A.H.

J.D. Hudson
Lt Col 2?1
Commanding 21st Div Amn Col

WAR DIARY
or
INTELLIGENCE SUMMARY.
(Erase heading not required.) 21st DIVL. AMMN. COL.

Army Form C. 2118

DEC?

Place	Date	Hour	Summary of Events and Information	Remarks and references to Appendices
ST. JAN CAPPEL	5/12/15	9am	1 Serjt, 1 Artily Bomdr, 1 Shoesynith, 1 Gunner, 10 Drivers, 8 G.S. Wagons, 20 L.D. Horses (including 1 Spare Wheel) + 2 Riding Horses proceeded by march route to CAMPAGNE when they joined 55th Divisional Ammunition Column.	OSF

J.D. Anderson Lt Col.
Commanding 21st Divl. Ammn. Col.

21st Divisional Artillery.

21st DIVISIONAL AMMUNITION COLUMN R. F. A.

JANUARY 1916.

Army Form C. 2118.

WAR DIARY
or
INTELLIGENCE SUMMARY.

(Erase heading not required.) 21ST DIVISIONAL AMMUNITION COLUMN

Place	Date	Hour	Summary of Events and Information	Remarks and references to Appendices
SEJAN CAPPEL	31st January 1916		There is nothing of interest to record during the month of January 1916. The unit occupied billets as in previous month.	

J.D. Anderson Lieut. R.F.A.
Commanding 21st Divisional Ammunition Col.

21st Divisional Artillery.

21st DIVISIONAL AMMUNITION COLUMN R. F. A.

FEBRUARY 1916.

Army Form C. 2118.

WAR DIARY
or
INTELLIGENCE SUMMARY. 21st DIVISIONAL AMMUNITION COLUMN
(Erase heading not required.)

Instructions regarding War Diaries and Intelligence Summaries are contained in F.S. Regs., Part II. and the Staff Manual respectively. Title pages will be prepared in manuscript.

Place	Date	Hour	Summary of Events and Information	Remarks and references to Appendices
CAPPEL	29/2/16		There is nothing to record during the month of February 1916.	[initials]

[signature]
Capt
Lt Col. R.F.A.
Commanding 21st Divl Ammn Coln

21st Divisional Artillery.

21st DIVISIONAL AMMUNITION COLUMN R.F.A.

M A R C H 1916.

Army Form C. 2118.

WAR DIARY
2/1st DIVISIONAL AMMUNITION COLUMN
INTELLIGENCE SUMMARY.

(Erase heading not required.)

Instructions regarding War Diaries and Intelligence Summaries are contained in F.S. Regs., Part II. and the Staff Manual respectively. Title pages will be prepared in manuscript.

Place	Date	Hour	Summary of Events and Information	Remarks and references to Appendices
NIEPPE	24/3/16	9 a.m.	ADVANCED (No 3) SECTION moved from NIEPPE to LA CRECHE on its being taken over by 17 DIVISIONAL ARTILLERY.	May
LA CRECHE	26/3/16	9.15 a.m.	No 3 SECTION moved from LA CRECHE to BORRE.	
			All Corps and Army working parties belonging to the column rejoined the unit previous to move of the division elsewhere.	WR
			In accordance with instructions from Head Quarters 1st February status hereof of transport vehicles & ammunition effects are another origins and transport vehicles.	WG
			18 Pdr – 56 G.S. Wagons
4.5 (How)   – 9   –"–
J.A.A.   – 20 –"–
Gun cars   – 1
Total 86 Wagons	

J. Tudworth Lt R.A.
Comdg 2/1st Div Amm Col

21st Divisional Artillery.

21st DIVISIONAL AMMUNITION COLUMN R.F.A.

A P R I L   1916.

Army Form C. 2118.

Vol 8

WAR DIARY
or
INTELLIGENCE SUMMARY.
(Erase heading not required.)

2nd DIVISIONAL AMM. COLN.

Instructions regarding War Diaries and Intelligence Summaries are contained in F. S. Regs., Part II. and the Staff Manual respectively. Title pages will be prepared in manuscript.

Place	Date	Hour	Summary of Events and Information	Remarks and references to Appendices
SUZANNE CAPPEL	14/4/16	6am	1st & 3rd M.T. SECTION proceed by march route to LONGUEAU.	
			On arrival at the latter place the proceed by train on to BUSSEY and DAOURS and on arrival went into bivouac at above places	W.E.
	14/4/16	6am	3rd M.T. Section proceed by march route to LONGUEAU and went into billets at BUSSEY and DAOURS	W.E.
BUSSEY	24/4/16		3rd M.T. 3 sections proceed to GODEWAERSVELDE	W.E.
			GODEWAERSVELDE	
SUZAN CAPPEL	21/4/16	6am	3rd M.T. Section & Sig. N. & other personnel remaining of Divisional Amm. Coln.	W.E.
			left, using 78 horses supplied by 8th D.A.C. proceeded to	
BUSSEY DAOURS	14/4/16	9am	1st & 2nd section proceed to DIVISIONAL SECTION to BUSSEY for L'ANCRE	W.E.
	19/4/16	10am	Remainder of Column moved to DRAUCOURT by rail and billets made by 9th BRIGADE R.F.A.	W.E.

J. Anderson R.F.A.
Commanding 2nd D.A. Column R.F.A.

2353 Wt. W3544/1484 700,000 5/15 D.D.&L. A.D.S.S./Forms/C.2118

21st Divisional Artillery.

21ST DIVISIONAL AMMUNITION COLUMN R.F.A.

M A Y 1916.

Army Form C. 2118.

Vol 4

WAR DIARY
or
INTELLIGENCE SUMMARY.
(Erase heading not required.)

21 DIVISIONAL COL. U.M.N.

L 16 C ?

Place	Date	Hour	Summary of Events and Information	Remarks and references to Appendices
BUIRE	11/5/16		The unit was reorganised & divided into 2 Echelons (A & B). 'A' Echelon was formed by absorbing the existing Brigade Ammunition Column of 94 95 + 96 Brigades R.F.A. The 97 Brigade Ammunition Column was distributed as a unit, the personnel in men + horses for the most part being absorbed into the 3 Sections of 'A' Echelon. 94 Bde Amn Col became No 1 Section 95 " " " " No 2 Section 96 " " " " No 3 Section The Establishment of each Section in 'A' Echelon became as follows:— 3 Officers + 168 other ranks with 19 Riding + 194 L.D. Horses + 33 vehicles. No 2 Section was at at the time of re-organisation was carrying out the functions of ADVANCED SECTION formed the nucleus upon which 'B' Echelon was formed. Surplus details of No 1 + 3 Section 21st Divisional Ammunition Column, after supply of 'B' Echelon to present War Estab being sent to ADVANCED HORSE TRANSPORT DEPOT ABBEVILLE, or front units orders of Divisional Artillery to make good wastage	WB

WAR DIARY
INTELLIGENCE SUMMARY
Army Form C. 2118.

Place	Date	Hour	Summary of Events and Information	Remarks and references to Appendices
BUIRE	1/6/16		Footage. The establishment of 'B' Echelon became as follows:— 4 Officers, 256 other ranks, 21 Riding + 310 L.D animals, and 479 S. Wagons. Surplus officers transport upon this reorganisation were disposed of by means of G.O6. R.A. 21st Division. The establishment of Ammunition Grenades carried became:—	G05
				With Battery 'A' Echelon 'B' Echelon Total in Division	
			18 Pdr rounds per gun 176 76 27 13392.	
			4.5 inch rounds per gun 108 48 66. 2664 (6.12 Hows)	
			S.A.A. 1,008,000. 832,000 1,840,000.	
			Grenades 4140 1380 5,520	
	29/5/16		The Corps Commander (B.Genl. H.L. Anne CB) inspected this unit. J.D. Anderson Lt Col R.A. Commanding 21st Divisional Column	

Adjutant General's Office
  Base
  ———

Herewith War diary of the unit under my
Command for the month of May 1916.

2/6/16

J. D. Anderson
Lieut Col ADMS
Comdg No. ? Divisional Colm

21st Divisional Artillery.

War Diary missing

21st DIVISIONAL AMMUNITION COLUMN R. F. A.

JUNE 1916.

21st Divisional Artillery.

21st DIVISIONAL AMMUNITION COLUMN R. F. A.

JULY 1916

WAR DIARY
or
INTELLIGENCE SUMMARY.
(Erase heading not required.)

Army Form C. 2118.

21 July

21st DIVISIONAL COLUMN.

Vol II

Place	Date	Hour	Summary of Events and Information	Remarks and references to Appendices
BUIRE	7/7/16		1. The dump at D.30.d.5.7 was further supplemented. The dump also captured & replenished the previous dump established at E.5.c.7.7 which supplied batteries located in L. BECOURT area. The decauville Railway carried the ammunition from the dumps to the N of BECOURT WOOD. A bringing party of 1 N.C. Officer & 12 men had been trained in helping arrivals, the party was heard under orders to proceed under an Officer & 21/94 in advance of that but on a move forward being made. 2 G.S. Wagons with 4 Runips to bridge the German front line trenches are kept in readiness.	Reference French Sheet 62 D.N.E.
MEAULTE	8/7/16	6 am	A dump was established at E.18.A.3.5., the batteries having moved forward the dump at E.5.c.7.7 was exhausted & abandoned. Ammunition was received direct from railheads, G.S. Wagons & & Carrs & Cars & advanced destinations being employed in carrying ammunition from the trains to dumps.	

Army Form C. 2118.

WAR DIARY
or
INTELLIGENCE SUMMARY.
(Erase heading not required.)

21st DIVISIONAL COLUMN

Place	Date	Hour	Summary of Events and Information	Remarks and references to Appendices
MEAULTE	8/9/16	—	M.M. DUMP was allotted to ammunition needed to the Corps and no all times of ammunition were made daily by A. Corps.	WG
"	16/9/16		Motor Lorries Commenced to carry ammunition from train to dump from 12 Noon to 8 today	WG
"	20/9/16		A dump was established at F.4.a.1.0 ammunition being carried forward up to E.18.a.3.3	WG
			3rd Brigade being supplied from the Somme + the remaining 3 by the latter.	
FRICOURT	23/9/16	8pm	Dumps at F.4.a.1.0 and E.18.a.3.3 handed on to 51 DIVL ARTILLERY	WG
			The following ammunition was handed on	
			At F.4.a.1.0 At E.18.a.3.3	
			A 12,064 A 7736	
			Ax 3375 Ax 8712	
			Bx 1766 Bx 1210	

Army Form C. 2118.

WAR DIARY
or
INTELLIGENCE SUMMARY.
(Erase heading not required.)

21st DIVISIONAL COLUMN

Place	Date	Hour	Summary of Events and Information	Remarks and references to Appendices
VILLER MILL	25/7/16	1pm	The unit (less RQA Section which had already moved) proceeded by march and GARGOEUVES arriving there at 8am on 26/7/16 and went into billets.	
	26/7/16	6am	The unit took in BUIRE, RIBEMONT, HEILLY, BONNAY, DAOURS, VECQUEMONT, AMIENS (skirting the city) and LONGPRÉ.	
ARGOEUVES	27/7/16	11:30am	The unit continued its march via St SAVEUR, LA CHAUSSEE, BELLOY-YLEUX. — arriving at BOURDON at 1pm where it went into billets.	
BOURDON			The march was continued via FLIXECOURT, MOUFLIERS, AILLY-L-HAUT CLOCHER, to St RIQUIER arriving there at 2pm where [illegible] the unit bivouacs. — The following day (28th) the unit went into St RIQUIER.	

Army Form C. 2118.

WAR DIARY
or
INTELLIGENCE SUMMARY.
(Erase heading not required.)

21st DIVISIONAL COLUMN

Place	Date	Hour	Summary of Events and Information	Remarks and references to Appendices
RIQUICR	29/7/16	5 am	Unit moved to WAVENS via COULONVILLERS – LONG VILLERS – DOMLEGER – MAIZICOURT – BEAUVOIS – RIVIERE arriving there at 10 am + rested for the night	WD
WAVANS	30/7/16	5 am	Unit continued its march via VILLERS – L'HOPITAL – BONNIERES – REBREUVIETTE to BERLENCOURT arriving at 10 am. The unit bivouacked in the East of the village + rested there on 31st July/16	WD

J. Anderson
Lt Col RAA
Comdg 21st Divl Column

2353 Wt. W2544/1454 700,000 5/15 D.D.&L. A.D.S.S./Forms/C.2118.

Headquarters,
   21st Divisional Artillery

Herewith War diary for this unit for
the month of July.

1/8/16

W. Gumbert
for OC 21st Divl Coln

21st Divisional Artillery.

21st DIVISIONAL AMMUNITION COLUMN R. F. A.

A U G U S T 1916.

WAR DIARY or INTELLIGENCE SUMMARY.

Army Form C. 2118.

Vol 72

21st DIVISIONAL AMMUNITION COLUMN

(Erase heading not required.)

Instructions regarding War Diaries and Intelligence Summaries are contained in F. S. Regs., Part II. and the Staff Manual respectively. Title pages will be prepared in manuscript.

Place	Date	Hour	Summary of Events and Information	Remarks and references to Appendices
BERLAN-COURT.	3/8/16	5-30 am	The Column proceeded by march route via LIENCOURT — AVESNES-LE-COMPTE to MONTENESCOURT where it billetted and reported the S.A.A. Section	WBG
	10/8/16		2,000 Rds of 18 Pdr Ammunition found to be surplus to establishment on taking over its line was returned to AMMUNITION SUB-PARK	WBG
	18/8/16		2 Brigades of 37 Divisional Artillery came under the orders of G.O.C. R.A. 21st Division. Ammunition for these guns was taken over from 37 Divisional Ammunition Column. The whole of ammunition held for guns was charged at the gun position, i.e. all echelons from Battery Wagon Line to Sub Park were taken to gun position. The system of supply was changed. Brigade H.Q. demanded their expenditure of previous 24 hours which was issued from railhead and coming under the orders of the R.F.A. Brigade Commander.	WBG
	26/9/16		A list of Ammunition Supply was made by Army H.Q. and the case of an emergency. At 9 a.m. a message was received to report 8/95 Bde RFA which means that 1446 Rds of Ammunition was required. As the Ammunition came up by 1 lorry only, next as it was not possible to send wagons from line of fire 1-45 am - 6 Ammunition Wagons only were able to be sent. The 3rd lorry has arrived at 2 a.m.	WBG

J. Anderson
Captain
21st D.A.C.

SITUATION 13.8.16. 125 Bde RFA   Maps1/10 36 B SE 4
On handing over to 52-d Bde RFA.   1/10 36 C SW 3
   A/52, B/125 to B/52, C/125 to C/52, D/125 to D/52, 9th Divn.

	A/125	B/125	C/125	D/125
Positions.	X 4 C 5-3	X 4 C 5-5	X 3 A 95-60	X 3 D 7-8
Zones.	S9 C 15-80 IRISH-CRATER to S 8 B 9-1	S 8 B 9-1 to S 9 A 15-80	S 9 A 15-80 to S 2 D 9-9	S 15 A 3-7 to S 2 D 9-9.
OPs normal	X 5 D 0-3	X 5D 0-3	X 5 D 2-7	X 5 D 2-7 near.
OPs Battle	X 10 C 85-05 not-made	X 10 D 6-2 not made	X 5 B 3-3 Being made	X 8 D 9-7 not made.
SOS	(1)S 9 C 32-80	S 9 A 00-30	S 9 A 3-7	S 15 A 85-87
	(2)S 9 C 30-95	S 9 A 05-45	S 3 C 20-05	S 9 C 80-55
	(3)S 9 A 25-02	S 9 A 10-65	S 3 C 15-25	S 9 A 82-50
	(4)S 9 A 25-11	S 9 A 10-60	S 2 D 98-60	S 9 A 50-90.
Code names HQ SHAVE	LATHER	TOWEL	STROP	SOAP
Some wire labels	1GCR	2 GCR	3 GCR	4 GCR
Extreme Arcs.	S 22 A 0-0 to S 3 C 0-5 120-89 true	S 22 A 6-5 to S 2 B 3-9 120-80 true	S 22 D 4-3 to M 32 B 3-0 118-82 true	S 22/C 1-9 to M 32 D 1-5 122-77 true.

(For extremes to help Divns on flanks, see 125/245 attached.)

Altern Posns	X 3 C 9-4?		R 33 C 2-7?	X 3 B 7-5
Dummy posns.		X 4 C 4-8?		X 3 D 3-9?
Infantry	Centre Battln	LEft Battln	Left Battln	Centre & Left.

Each battery in turn finds an Officer for LEFT Battaln HQ at night.
   & a telephone man by day & night.
Officer for CENTRE BATTALN HQ comes from 126 Bde RFA.
A & B find alternately an Officer for OP on LORETTE & C & D one who
     sleep at OP by night.
(Visual)
 Stations.) receives signals by lamp or flag from LEFT BTN HQ at S 8 B
HQ X 8 D 8-8)   2-3 & signals to 125 Bde HQ at X 2 B 5-3 &
     to near each battery. About/ At X 8 D 8-8 are lamp BOXES
     pointed at 125 Hq, & at each battery. Near it is also an
     old CP for Battle.
LEFT GROUP COMDR is at X 7 D 1-1. Rt Group Comdr at X28 A 4-7.
  ZONE. The Divnl Sector is divided into 3 sections, BERTHONVAL(with 2
     subsections) & CARENCY (CARENCY I,II,II subsections.)
     125 deals with CARENCY II (1 battery)& III(2 batteries 18pr).
     For Boundaries see C/101/62 attached.
    The LEFT of CARENCY III is considered (by other than Battaln Cmdr)
     as much safer than th area by the NORTHERN MINE SYSTEM. This
     SYSTEM requires careful firing. Near edges of craters are held
     by us, far by enemy. It is not safe to fire at craters.
 FLANKS. On South(Right) 60th Divn. On NORTH(Left)63 R N Divn.
     On getting message "DEFEND SOUCHEZ,"B/125 barrages S 3 A 4-3,
     to S 3 C 4-3, C & D/125 barrage S 3 A 45-20 to S 3 C 90-75.
     see also C/101/72 in File "Help for Flank Divns".

war diary
WbsNo5.

21st Divisional Artillery.

21st DIVISIONAL AMMUNITION COLUMN R. F. A.

SEPTEMBER 1916

WAR DIARY
or
INTELLIGENCE SUMMARY.

(Erase heading not required.)

Army Form C. 2118.

Place	Date	Hour	Summary of Events and Information	Remarks and references to Appendices
MONTEN ESCOURT	9/9/16	6am	The Column left for Drumont Drouvry & proceeded by march route to RIZIENSTEET BROUILLY. Nos. 2, 3 & 4 Sections together with Headquarters being Billeted in former place & No 1 Section at the latter.	
WARMIN	10/9/16	10.30a	I.M. Brigade arrived from ARRAS and were billeted in the area.	
ROZIERES	12/9/16	7am	Left for 15th Corps Area (in IVERGNY, LUCHEUX, GALLOY, VACQUELLES) where the column rested for the night.	
VAUCHELLES	12/9/16	6.30 am	Left VAUCHELLES and returned the whole of LEALVILLERS, SENLIS to ALBERT and encamped at BECK'S WE FARM	
ALBERT	13/9/16	6pm	1 Officer & 50 men left for CHOCILLOT FARM encountered camp and Headqrs 'B' & no 6 Section to Quarenters Setup	

… Army Form C. 2118.

Vol 3

WAR DIARY
or
INTELLIGENCE SUMMARY.

21st DIVISIONAL AMMUNITION COLN

(Erase heading not required.)

Place	Date	Hour	Summary of Events and Information	Remarks and references to Appendices
ALBERT	14/6/16		The Divisional Artillery on a whole are constantly to get this Unit as an ammunition are received through this Division	
MAMETZ	14/6/16		W/2 Section proceeded on an Ammunition Column up a position at F.6.a.	
			(ALBERT-COMBINED SHEET)	
	15/6/16 9pm		Remainder of Column (less "B" Echelon) proceeded to MAMETZ + took up position near No 2 Section	

J Mulcaster
For A.D.A
Commanding 21st Divl Amm Col

21st Divisional Artillery.

21st DIVISIONAL AMMUNITION COLUMN R. F. A.

OCTOBER 1 9 1 6

OCTOBER

Army Form C. 2118.

WAR DIARY
or
INTELLIGENCE SUMMARY.

Vol 14

(Erase heading not required.)

Instructions regarding War Diaries and Intelligence Summaries are contained in F.S. Regs., Part II. and the Staff Manual respectively. Title pages will be prepared in manuscript.

Place	Date	Hour	Summary of Events and Information	Remarks and references to Appendices
MAMETZ	1/10/16		"B" Bttn. "B" was detached from the Column & proceeded by Motor Bus with the ammunition (who was going to a new part of the line).	
"	8/10/16		"B" Echelon rejoined the Column.	
"	9/10/16		A new ammunition dump was formed at BAZENTIN le PETIT. From this dak fresh animals were sent for ammunition supply instead of wagons on account of the bad roads.	
"	15/10/16	7.30 am	The Column marched out & proceeded by Motor route to LA NEUVILLE	
LA NEUVILLE	16/10/16		March was continued to TALMAS	
TALMAS	17/10/16		" " ORVILLE	
ORVILLE	18/10/16		" " LIGNY SUR CANCHE area VACQUERIE BRIDGE	
LIGNY-SUR-CANCHE	19/10/16		" " ANVIN - from here an officer was sent forward to take over billets from 1st DAC	
ANVIN	20/10/16		" " LABREUVIERE - at which place two coods.	

2353. Wt. W3544/1454 700,000 5/15 D. D. & L. A.D.S.S./Forms/C. 2118.

WAR DIARY
or
INTELLIGENCE SUMMARY
(Erase heading not required.)

Place	Date	Hour	Summary of Events and...
LABEY...	2/9/16		March continued to first destination...

21st Divisional Artillery

21st DIVISIONAL AMMUNITION COLUMN R. F. A

NOVEMBER 1916.

Army Form C. 2118.

WAR DIARY
or
INTELLIGENCE SUMMARY.

21st DIVISIONAL AMMUNITION COLUMN

(Erase heading not required.)

Instructions regarding War Diaries and Intelligence Summaries are contained in F. S. Regs., Part II and the Staff Manual respectively. Title pages will be prepared in manuscript.

Place	Date	Hour	Summary of Events and Information	Remarks and references to Appendices
			There is nothing of note to record for the month of NOVEMBER	
			[signature] Lieut Col 21st Divisional Ammn Co.	

21st Divisional Artillery.

21st DIVISIONAL AMMUNITION COLUMN R. F. A.

DECEMBER 1916.

Army Form C.—

WAR DIARY
or
INTELLIGENCE SUMMARY.

21st Divisional Column

Army Form C. 2118.

WAR DIARY
or
INTELLIGENCE SUMMARY.
(Erase heading not required.)

21st DIVISIONAL AMMUNITION COLUMN

Vol 17

Instructions regarding War Diaries and Intelligence Summaries are contained in F.S. Regs. Part II. and the Staff Manual respectively. Title pages will be prepared in manuscript.

Place	Date	Hour	Summary of Events and Information	Remarks and references to Appendices
VERQUIGNEUL	5/1/17	9.30 am	The unit moved into 1st Corps Rest area. No 1, 2 & 3 Sections with Headquarters being billeted at ANNEZIN and "B" Echon at HESIDGNEUL.	
ANNEZIN	14/1/17		Orders received to reorganise the Column. No 3 Section was disbanded, the personnel and equipment being divided between 6th & 24th Divisional Artillery, also sufficient vehicles & horses to No 1 & 2 Sections to expand to 6 Gun Batteries. CAPTAIN A. BOTTING was posted to 24 R.A. A.C. The abution of 9 euro were absorbed in No 1 & 2 Sections.	
ANNEZIN	28/1/17		Orders received to march at 9am to new area. The unit marched via EHOQUES LILLERS – St VENANT – MERVILLE & NEUF-BERQUIN – VIEUX-BERQUIN area and billetes for the night at GAUDESCURE.	REFERENCE SHEET 5A 1/100,000
GAUDESCURE	29/1/17	9am	March continued via VIEUX-BERQUIN – STRAZEELE – CAISTRE – EECKE – STEENVOORDE to HERZEELE where the unit went into billets.	

J.D. Anderson
Comdg 21st Divl Ammn Col.

A.D.S.S./Forms/C. 2118.

21st Div Am Col

WAR DIARY
or
INTELLIGENCE SUMMARY.
(Erase heading not required.)

Army Form C. 2118.

31st Divisional Ammunition Column   Vol 18

Place	Date	Hour	Summary of Events and Information	Remarks and references to Appendices
HERZEELE	10/2/17	8.15 am	Orders having been received to march to 1st Corps Area. The unit proceed by march route to HAZEBROUCK (via STEENVOORDE) where it was billeted for the night	WBG
HAZEBROUCK	15/2/17	9 am	The march was continued via ST VENANT — ROBECQ — Mt BERNENCHON to RIEN-DU-VINAGE where the column rested on 14th & 15th February	WBG
RIEN-DU-VINAGE	16/2/17	8 am	The unit completed its march to VERQUIGNEUL proceeding via VENDIN-LES-BETHUNE — BETHUNE. 'B' Echelon pivoted to BEUVRY. The relief of 62nd Divisional Ammn Column was completed & supply of ammunition taken over to 12am (Noon) on this date. 38th A.F.A. Bde R.Cs was attached for purpose of ammunition supply. Reference HAZEBROUCK 1/100,000 SHEET 5A.	WBG

W B Gunter? Major
OC 31st Divisional Ammn Column

WAR DIARY
or
INTELLIGENCE SUMMARY.

(Erase heading not required.)

Army Form C. 2118.

Vol 19

21st Divisional Ammunition Column

Instructions regarding War Diaries and Intelligence Summaries are contained in F. S. Regs., Part II. and the Staff Manual respectively. Title pages will be prepared in manuscript.

Place	Date	Hour	Summary of Events and Information	Remarks and references to Appendices
VERQUIGNEUL	5/3/17	12 Noon	The Column was relieved by 6th Divisional Ammunition Column & the supply of ammunition for the CAMBRIN - HOHENZOLLERN - QUARRIES - GROUPS - were taken over at 12 noon	
RIEN-DU-VINAGE	11/3/17	8 am	The unit (less No 2 Section & proportion of B' Echelon who remained in the line with 110 Bty Bde & 95 Bde RFA) proceeded by march route to RIEN-DU-VINAGE where it rested from 5th to 10th inclusive. The unit marched to 3rd Army Area (7th Corps) & proceeded via GONNEHEM - LILLERS - S't HILAIRE - to HEUCHIN when it rested the night following day.	
HEUCHIN	13/3/17	9-30 am	The march was continued via ANVIN to AUBROMETZ where the night was spent	
AUBROMETZ	14/3/17	8-30 am	March continued via BOUBERS-SUR-CANCHE - FREVENT - BONNIERES - BARLY where owing to the bad state of the roads the Column was halted for the night.	
BARLY	15/3/17	7-30 am	Unit proceeded via OCCHES - DOULLENS to LUCHEUX where it was encamped for the night	
LUCHEUX	16/3/17	12 Noon	The unit came under the orders of 30 Divisional Artillery for Ammunition Supply & proceeded via SOMBRIN - BARLY - FOSSEUX to GOUY-EN-ARTOIS where it received by the wagon line	

Army Form C. 2118.

WAR DIARY
or
INTELLIGENCE SUMMARY. (Contd.)

(Erase heading not required.)

21st DIVISIONAL AMMUNITION COLUMN

Instructions regarding War Diaries and Intelligence Summaries are contained in F.S. Regs., Part II and the Staff Manual respectively. Title pages will be prepared in manuscript.

Place	Date	Hour	Summary of Events and Information	Remarks and references to Appendices
			Lives & hicuts of 30th Divisional Ammunition Column who went forward.	
GUOY-EN-ARTOIS	23/5/17	2 p.m.	The unit came under the orders of 56th Divisional Artillery and proceeded to a camp at MONCHIET situated at Q.21.c.0.5 (Ref. Sheet 51c)	W/B
			All ammunition in Echelon was dumped at Gun positions, the unit also fetching Gun rounds from pits. Similar work continued on the nights of 24th & 25th inst.	
MONCHIET	27/5/17	3 p.m.	No.2 Section & portion of B. Echelon rejoins Gun Park Army Area	W/B
"	28/5/17	9 a.m.	The Column (less No.3 Section) moved to a camp at BAILLEULMONT where it came under the orders of its own Divisional Artillery. The unit was situated as follows:- H.Q. Gp. W.8.c.0.7.) Return No.1 Sec. N.3.c.) Sheet N.2 Sec. W.9.a. + W.8.d.) 51c.	W/B
			20 Officers + 50 men proceeded to ADINFER & then took over the dump at X.21.d.6.5 (Ref. Sheet 51c)	
"	31/5/17	9 a.m.	No.3 Section moved to a camp at X.7.a. central (Ref. Sheet 57) near RANSART.	W/B

W.T. Anderson
Lieut Col.
Commanding 21st Divl. Ammn. Col.

Army Form C. 2118.

WAR DIARY
or
INTELLIGENCE SUMMARY.

(Erase heading not required.)

21st DIVL. AMMN COLUMN   Vol 21

Place	Date	Hour	Summary of Events and Information	Remarks and references to Appendices
BOYELLES	16/5/17	9 am	'A' Echelon with Headquarters went to form position at BOIRY St RICTRUDE at about S19 b (Ref: Sheet 51.B) Where a dump was constructed. 'B' Echelon went to a position at about N 22 (a) (Ref: Sheet 51.H) near ADINFER	

N. Anderson
Lieut Col. R.F.A.
Commanding 21st Divl Ammn Coln

Army Form C. 2118.

WAR DIARY
or
INTELLIGENCE SUMMARY.

(Erase heading not required.) 21st DIVISIONAL AMMUNITION COLUMN   Vol 20

Instructions regarding War Diaries and Intelligence Summaries are contained in F. S. Regs., Part II. and the Staff Manual respectively. Title pages will be prepared in manuscript.

Place	Date	Hour	Summary of Events and Information	Remarks and references to Appendices
BAILLEUL	9/4/17	6 am	The Column moved to a farm in S.19.a. (Refs Sheet 51B.) S.W. of BOIRY St RICTRUDE	WGF
MONT ST	10/4/17	6 am	The Column of 'a' Echelon moved ammunition direct to gun positions	WGF
	11/4/17		A dump was formed near ST VAAST near BOIRY St RICTRUDE when batteries of 12" & 58th Divisional Artillery moved their Supplies	WGF
BOIRY St R	12/4/17		Dump at ADINFER closed & details working there rejoined the unit	WGF
RICTRUDE	20/4/17		37th Divisional Artillery attached us, relief of 58th D.A.	WGF
	21/4/17	9 am	Dump formed at BOYELLES for supply of 21st & 37th DIVISIONAL ARTILLERY	WGF
	22/4/17	9 am	No 1 & 2 Sections moved to a farm at BOYELLES at S.18.b.75 (S18.b.75)	WGF
	23/4/17	9 am	Hd Qs & No 3 Section moved to BOYELLES at S.18.b.75	WGF

J. Anderson ?Lieut
Comg 21st D.A.C.

2353 W₁ W2511/2454 700,000 5/15 D. D. & L.   A.D.S.S./Forms/C. 2118.

Army Form C. 2118.

WAR DIARY
or
INTELLIGENCE SUMMARY.
(Erase heading not required.)

Vol XXII

2nd Divisional Ammunition Column

Place	Date	Hour	Summary of Events and Information	Remarks and references to Appendices
BOIRY St. RICTRUDE	22/6/17 to 7/11 Nov		33rd Divisional Artillery took over the dumps at SUCERIE, BOIRY St. RICTRUDE.	

W. Armstrong Lt. Col. OC.
for OC. 2nd DAC.

Army Form C. 2118.

WAR DIARY
or
INTELLIGENCE SUMMARY.

(Erase heading not required.) 31st Divisional Ammunition Column

Vol 23

Place	Date	Hour	Summary of Events and Information	Remarks and references to Appendices
BORRY & RICHEBOURG	1/2/17	12 Noon	Drunk at SUCRERIE taken over from 33rd Divisional Artillery	WD
	19/2/17	12 Noon	New dump established at BUSSY — BEQUE BELLE at S12.b. Ref. Sheet 5 s.w. 1/20,000	AP

J.D. Tuckworth
Sailor R.E.A
Commanding 31st Division A.C.

Army Form C. 2118.

WAR DIARY
or
INTELLIGENCE SUMMARY.
(Erase heading not required.)

2nd DIVl. AMMN. COLUMN.

Vol 24

Place	Date	Hour	Summary of Events and Information	Remarks and references to Appendices
BOIRY, BECQUER-ELLE	22/8/17		Dump at S.12.d. (Reference Sheet 57B 1/20,000) relinquished & dump at S.19.a.6.6. м BOYELLES — BAPAUME ROAD established.	WB
	23rd August 1917		The Column was re-organised under orders from G.H.Q. "B" Echelon became the S.A.A. Section & was distributing with ammunition for the Infantry Brigades. Nº 1 & 2 Sections carry 18 Pdr & 4.5" Hows Ammunition. This re-organisation reduces the number of vehicles in the unit by 1 Maltese Cart & 188 Wagons. All vehicles other than those allotted for the carriage of Guns or their Ammunition are now drawn by & animals instead of 6, as hitherto. The number of Animals on the establishment of the unit are now:—	WB

	Riding	Draught	Total
Head Qr.	11	32	43
Nº 1 Sec.	21	228	249
Nº 2 Sec.	21	228	249
S.A.A. Sec.	20	176	196
	73	664	737

W. Winhel Barton
for O.C. 2nd Divl. Am. Col.

2353 W¹: W25+t/1454 700,000 5/15 D.D.&L. A.D.S.S./Forms/C. 2118.

Army Form C. 2118.

Vol 25

WAR DIARY
or
INTELLIGENCE SUMMARY.
(Erase heading not required.)

21st DIVL. AMMN COLUMN

Place	Date	Hour	Summary of Events and Information	Remarks and references to Appendices
BOIRY. St RICTRUDE	5/9/17	—	The unit entrained at AUBIGNY — ARRAS (A+B) by sections in the transport of 21 Div Arty to 2nd Army (X Corps). H.Q. + S.A. Section entrained at AUBIGNY. No 1 Sect. at ARRAS (A) + No 2 Section at ARRAS (B)	WG
HOPOUTRE GODEWAERSVELDE CAESTRE	6/9/17	2pm	21st D.A.C. detrained at Stations shown + proceeded to billets near THIEUSHAUK, about H.Q. + No 1 + No 2 E in CAESTRE (Rfee HAZEBROUCK)	WG
"	14/9/17	6am	Left billets on above + proceeded by march route to RENINGHELST, when the unit encamped. H.Q. at G 35, c, 2, 7. S.A.A. Section at G 35, c, 8, 5, No 1 Section at M 6 b 5 when the No 2 Section also encamped	WG
RENINGHELST AREA	16/9/17	—	2 Officers + 40 other ranks proceeded to work on dump at N 4 c, 5, 3, entrucks by 4th D.A.	WG
—	30/9/17	6am	The unit took over control of JELLICOE DUMP, situate at H 26, 6, 0, 7. The A.R.P. supplies 21st D.A, further, 1 Bde of 4th D.A + 315 A.F.A. Brigade	WG

Army Form C. 2118.

WAR DIARY
or
INTELLIGENCE SUMMARY.
(Erase heading not required.)

Place	Date	Hour	Summary of Events and Information	Remarks and references to Appendices
			Owing to the nature of ground covered in supply of ammunition, the war of pack equipment had to be resorted to. The 1st A.A. Section during the latter days of the month were engaged in carrying ammunition from A.R.P. to the village of HOOGE, from whence they carried it by pack animal to CLAPHAM JUNCTION. All references unless otherwise stated refer to SHEET 28. 1/40,000	MG

J.S. Henderson
Lieut A Co
Commanding 21st Div A Col

Army Form C. 2118.

Vol 26

21 DIVISIONAL AMMN. COLUMN

WAR DIARY
or
INTELLIGENCE SUMMARY.
(Erase heading not required.)

Place	Date	Hour	Summary of Events and Information	Remarks and references to Appendices
ZEVE COTEN	20/10/17	12 Noon	The unit two over the control of A.R.P. known as 'BEATTY' situate at about H.29.b.5.5. (Cap Berg) Sheet 28. 1/40,000.	

Army Form C. 2118.

WAR DIARY
or
INTELLIGENCE SUMMARY.
(Erase heading not required.)

21st DIVISIONAL AMMUNITION COLUMN Vol 27

Place	Date	Hour	Summary of Events and Information	Remarks and references to Appendices
CAFE BELGE	14/XI/17	12 (Noon)	Handed over to BEATTY. A.R.P. at H29.B.5.5. (Reference Sheet 28, 1/40,000)	WBG
RENING-HELST.	15/XI/17	8am	The unit proceeded to 1st Army Area by march route, and halted at MORBECQUE where it rested the nights 15/16 and 16/17.	WBG
MORBECQUE	17/XI/17	9-50 am	The 21st Divl Ammn Column continued its march via S.VENANT to ANNEZIN where it rested the night 17/18.	WBG
ANNEZIN	18/XI/17	10 am	The march was continued, the unit resting night 18/19 at OURTON.	WBG *
OURTON	19/XI/17	9am	The unit marched via HOUDAIN to OLHAIN where it went into rest billets the nights 19/20 and 20/21	WBG *
OLHAIN	21/XI/17	8am	The unit to 13th Corps, 1st Army was instructed the next relieving 47 D.A.C in the line + took over wagon lines at that unit at ANZIN-S.AUBIN. The A.R. Ps at G.11.d.5.8. (Sheet 51 B N.W.) was taken over at 12 (noon) on this date	WBG
ANZIN S.AUBIN	29/XI/17	3-30 am	The A.R.P. at G.11.d.5.8. (Sheet 51 B.N.W.) was handed over to 31st Divl Ammn Column.	WBG

⊕ Reference HAZEBROUCK 5A.
* Reference LENS 3, 11.

WBG Lieut Col
for OC 21 Divl Ammn Col

Army Form C. 2118.

WAR DIARY
or
INTELLIGENCE SUMMARY.

21st Divisional Ammunition Column

Dec 1917

(Erase heading not required.)

WA 28

Place	Date	Hour	Summary of Events and Information	Remarks and references to Appendices
Anzin	1/12/17	7.30 AM	The unit left ANZIN and proceeded to BEAUVENCOURT and rested through the night	
Beauvencourt	2/12/17	6.30 AM	The unit resumed the march and proceeded to BOUCLY & went into B camp S.	
	4/12/17	12 noon	A.R.P., under command of 2/Lt Coltman, mg. attacked at C.V. 18 being @	
Brigneques	8/12/17	9 AM	The unit moved to camp at TINCOURT WOOD. ✻	

@ MAP 62c J 30 A no ✻ MAP 62c H 1 Q 41 @ MAP 62 c E 2 d

E.V. Bauer 2/Lt
for O.C. 21st Div. Amm. Col.

Army Form C. 2118.

J/21 Heavy Trench Mortar Bty. WAR DIARY or INTELLIGENCE SUMMARY

(Erase heading not required.)

For January 1914.

T M Bty 21 Div

Vol 37

Place	Date	Hour	Summary of Events and Information	Remarks and references to Appendices
			During this period the Battery has been out of action. On 4-1-19 we left the Loos front and proceeded to C.4. (Sheet 36 B). On 28-1-19 the Battery left C.4. and proceeded to B.18 ("). On the morning of the 30-1-19 we left B.18 and proceeded to F.2.4.6 (Sheet 5A).	

J. M. Fulton Capt
OC J/21 T M Bty

WAR DIARY
or
INTELLIGENCE SUMMARY.

(Erase heading not required.)

Army Form C. 2118.

21st DIVISIONAL AMMUNITION COLUMN.

WA 29

Place	Date	Hour	Summary of Events and Information	Remarks and references to Appendices
TINCOURT WOOD	21/1/1918	8 AM	The unit moved and took up new quarters at DERNICOURT	

Army Form C. 2118.

WAR DIARY
or
INTELLIGENCE SUMMARY.
21st Divisional Ammunition Column
(Erase heading not required.)

Vol 30

Place	Date	Hour	Summary of Events and Information	Remarks and references to Appendices
DRIEKURT	14/10/16	8 am	S.A.A. Section moved to billets at LONGUENESSE at about E 25.A	

Army Form C. 2118.

VOL 31

WAR DIARY
or
INTELLIGENCE SUMMARY.
(Erase heading not required.)

3rd DIVISIONAL AMMUNITION COLUMN

Place	Date	Hour	Summary of Events and Information	Remarks and references to Appendices
DRIENCOURT	21/3/18		The German bombardment commenced at 4-30 am on DRIENCOURT followed by British heavy action.	
	22/3/18	10 am	In consequence of the German advance the Column retired to a position approximately J3.c. FOULLICOURT — ALLAINES — ROAD (Sheet 62c)	
	22/3/18	5 am	A further retirement was made at 5 am to a position at CLERY-SUR-SOMME (H5.d) (Sheet 62c) — At 10 am the unit moved N of HEM. (N8.a), and a further retirement was made at 3 pm. to BRAY-SUR-SOMME — via CURLU — MARICOURT — a position being taken up at L15.c. (Sheet 62D)	
BRAY SUR SOMME	23/3/18		In the night of 23/24 and 24/25 the unit bivouacs at BRAY-SUR-SOMME, leaving that place at 9 am for ETINEHEM (L9.a) (Sheet 62 D). At 10 pm on 25/3/18 a retirement was made to VAUX — SUR — SOMME — via CHIPILLY — SAILLY-LAURETTE — SAILLY — le SEC — and rested night 25/26 at about T26c (Sheet 62D) — At 8 am on 26/3/18 the unit left VAUX — and proceeded by MERICOURT — BRESLE — BAIZEAUX to CONTAY — and bivouac there on nights 26/27.	

2533. Wt. W3544/1454 700,000 5/15 D.D.&L. A.D.S.S./Forms/C. 2118.

WAR DIARY
INTELLIGENCE SUMMARY.
(Erase heading not required.)

Army Form C. 2118.

Place	Date	Hour	Summary of Events and Information	Remarks and references to Appendices
CONTAY	29/3/16	2pm	27/28 at V.27.n. (Sheet 57a) The unit left CONTAY and proceeded to a position at about B.8.g.t C.1.5.6.0.9. (Sheet 62a) <u>Summary</u> During the retirement from the position at HAUT-ALLAINES a number of ammunition wagons finding the batteries in action, their came under hostile shell fire - 15 18 Pdr and 3-4-5 Hows. Wagons were lost. The following casualties were incurred. - Killed 1 - Wounded 12, missing 6 - On the 26th. March - 14 L.G.S. Wagons were unable to proceed with Germans to an advanced position were threatened. - The Ammunition was destroyed but owing to hostile machine gun fire & positions intensity, the wagons had to be abandoned. - There was no possibility of retaining those wagons.	[signatures]

21st Divisional Artillery.

21st DIVISIONAL AMMUNITION COLUMN R.F.A. :

APRIL 1918.

Army Form C. 2118.

WAR DIARY
or
INTELLIGENCE SUMMARY.
(Erase heading not required.)

21st DIVISIONAL AMMUNITION COLUMN.   Vol 32

Instructions regarding War Diaries and Intelligence Summaries are contained in F.S. Regs., Part II and the Staff Manual respectively. Title pages will be prepared in manuscript.

Place	Date	Hour	Summary of Events and Information	Remarks and references to Appendices
BERENCOURT	28/3/16 to 6/4/18		The 21st DAC remained in Camp at BERENCOURT [57C.B.c.09] until April 6th 1918 when it moved to Camp at QUERRIEU	
QUERRIEU	6/4/18 to 12/4/18	10 a.m.	HQ's and No 1 section moving on April 6th and No 2 sec on April 8th [on AA section entrained from S.ROOM (AMIENS) on 11/4/18 for HOUDAINE Join to 21st Division]	
HEM	12/4/18 to 13/4/18	8 p.m.	On April 12th the unit (less AAsec) marches to HEM 3/4 and went into Camp at [57 A.B.b.11] and business was the 13/4/18. During the 13/4/18 unit entrained in lories for DOULLENS the last party leaving at 8 a.m. on 14/4/1918. Detachment of unit took place at GUIDRACOURT WIEZE and BEAUVRE from 7 am to 5.30 pm 14/4/18.	
ACHEUX	14/4/18 to 15/4/18		By night of 14/4/18 the unit dumped at [27 R 1 d 33] On 15/4/18 ARP established at [27 R 1 d 33]	
BECKE	18/4/18 to 30/4/19	9 a.m.	On 18/4/18 unit (less AA section) moved Camp to 27.Q.30.b.67. and ARP established at 27 Q 30 b 6.7. On 20/4/18 No 1 sec change camp and moved into 27.R.1.c.33 and established an ARP at same locality On 25/4/18 No 1 sec Q.19.c.3.7 On 30/4/18 AA sec changed camp from [28 G 22 c 8.7] to [27 L 19 a.03]	

D.V. Nairnow /4
a/Captain
21st Div Ann Col.

Army Form C. 2118.

WAR DIARY

~~INTELLIGENCE~~ SUMMARY

(Erase heading not required.)

2st Divisional Ammunition Column.

N.L. 33

Instructions regarding War Diaries and Intelligence Summaries are contained in F. S. Regs., Part II. and the Staff Manual respectively. Title pages will be prepared in manuscript.

Place	Date 1918	Hour	Summary of Events and Information	Remarks and references to Appendices
EECKE	May 1st May 3		In camp at EECKE. [Q 20.a.11.8] Sheet 27.	
ST. MOMELIN	May 4	7am	Left for ST MOMELIN [SAR at HERZEELE]	Sgd
ST. OMER ARQUES WIZERNES	May 5	10.07	DAC began entraining throughout the following day from ST. OMER ARQUES and WIZERNES	Sgd
	May 6			
BURLEGE SAVIGNY	May 6 May 7	6.30pm	DAC began detraining throughout Hospital Transport (6") and Savigny (J") at BURLEGE and SAVIGNY.	Sgd
AOUGNY	May 7	3pm	DAC ex. centri AOUGNY. [Soissons 22, 4I 7.3] DAC marched to CHATEAU du BOIS de l'ABBE [From 122, 4 K 18, 4 I 4.7]	Sgd
CHATEAU du BOIS DE L'ABBE	May 12	8pm	Arrival in new camp at 10pm.	Sgd
	May 15		N°2 Sect + SAR in camp near BOIS GUINHE. [Soissons 22, 3K 3.9]	
	May 17	8pm	Intense bombardment lasted all day into 9.0 attack in the early morning.	Sgd
VANDEUIL	May 27	11.0pm	Arrived VANDEUIL and camped in night. Left CHATEAU du BOIS de l'ABBE at 8pm for VANDEUIL [3J 53]	Sgd
	May 28	7.30pm	Left VANDEUIL and Column passing via Sergent via heavy shell and rifle and Barrage. Casualties 2 men wounded, 2 horses.	Sgd
STE ESPERANCE	May 29	3pm	Arrived STE ESPERANCE at 3pm. [4K 2.7]	Sgd
	May 29	9pm	Left STE ESPERANCE for LA NEUVILLE [5K 1.8]	Sgd
LA NEUVILLE	May 29	9pm	Arrived LA NEUVILLE and left at 7pm for S. DENIS (ST MARTERIO) [5L 08]	Sgd
ST DENIS	May 30	1am	Arrived S. DENIS and left at 2.30 pm for camp between OTHEGY and MARQUER an bivouac of ...	[From 12, 6K 8.7] Sgd

Signed .... Capt RFA
21 DAC 31/6

WAR DIARY
or
INTELLIGENCE SUMMARY. 21st DIVISIONAL AMMUNITION COLUMN

Army Form C. 2118. Vol 34

Place	Date	Hour	Summary of Events and Information	Remarks and references to Appendices
DNMERY	12/6/18	9am	Saw Section left to join Infantry & entrained under Lieutenant P.	
	13/6/18	8.30am	H.Q. No 1 & 2 Section moved to VAUXPRÉ	
VAUXPRÉ	14/6/18	7am	Head entrained to CONNANTRAY. No 2 Section being detailed with 95 Bde RFA	
			at NORMÉE	
	17/6/18	10am	Nos 1 Section moved to MAILLY-LES-CAMPS	
	18/6/18	6pm	The Column entrained at MAILLY-LES-CAMPS & SOUS-SOMME for 4th Army Rest	
	19/6/18	6pm	Area	
	19/6/18		Detrained at PONT REMY and LONGPRÉ	
	20/6/18			
	21/6/18		The Column concentrated at BOUTTENCOURT	

Army Form C. 2118.

WAR DIARY
or
INTELLIGENCE SUMMARY.

(Erase heading not required.)

31st MT Column K 7/1

Place	Date	Hour	Summary of Events and Information	Remarks and references to Appendices
BOUTTENCOURT	22/6/18	10am	Left for ST MARTIN-LE GAILLARD Area. H.Qrs. No 1 & 2 Sections at ST MARTIN. No 3 at St SULPICE.	
ST MARTIN LE GAILLARD AREA	30/6/18	9am	Column remains at BOUTTEN COURT where it rested	

30-6-18

R Dunbar Major
OC 31 MT Co

Army Form C. 2118.

WAR DIARY
or
INTELLIGENCE SUMMARY.
(Erase heading not required.)

21st Div Amm Col.
RTA
Vol 35

Place	Date	Hour	Summary of Events and Information	Remarks and references to Appendices
BOUTTENCOURT	July 1916		Column remained at BOUTTENCOURT until the morning of the 21st July.	
	21/7/16	9 am	Column proceeded to LIERCOURT and Langrune and N° 1 sections at Brig-last MAREUIL. N° 2 Section SAA dump at BEAUFONTAINES	
	22/7/16	8.30 am	Column proceeded to CANAPLES there being no rooms at WAGNIES	
	23/7/16	9.30 am	Column proceeded to RAINCHEVAL and ammunition to RAINECHEVAL.	
	26/7/16	3 pm	TARTENCOURT ROAD. SAA section at ARQUEVES	
			SAA section moved to O6.c (57D)	
	28/7/16	10.30 am	Headquarters and N° 2 Section moved to O11.c (57D)	
	29/7/16	10.30	Headquarters and N° 1 Section moved to O11.c (57D)	
	23/7/16	10 am	Column took over A.R.T. from 23rd Div dumps at O5E (57D)	

Hothersall Capt
acq 21st D.A.C

WAR DIARY
INTELLIGENCE SUMMARY

Army Form C. 2118.

Star "5th Army" Release

Vol 36

Place	Date	Hour	Summary of Events and Information	Remarks and references to Appendices
LEALVILLERS	21/7/18	2pm	Headquarters + No 1 & 2 Sections left camp at O.H.C. for position in forward area. S.A.A. Sect detached awaits orders from Q branch 21st Dn.	JC
MAILLY MAILLET	24/7/18		Column moved from 4pm to 7pm to the positions in MIRAUMONT area, entry through on the BEAUCOURT - MIRAUMONT Rd., head of Column at R4 c22	JC
BEAUCOURT SUR ANCRE	25/7/18	7.30 am	Column moved at 7.30am to ARTILLERY VALLEY at R7c	JC
"	24/7/18	8pm	Column proceeded to R5a central and encamped on track PETIT MIRAUMONT - PYS	JC
PYS	3/8/18	3pm	Column moved to M14 & NW of Le SARS.	JC
			During above period recon. A.R.P. were established under orders from Staff Capt 21st D.A.	JC

Holden Capt
Acting 21st D.A.C.

Army Form C. 2118.

21 D Au Cy
WD 37

WAR DIARY
or
INTELLIGENCE SUMMARY.
(Erase heading not required.)

Instructions regarding War Diaries and Intelligence Summaries are contained in F. S. Regs., Part II. and the Staff Manual respectively. Title pages will be prepared in manuscript.

Place	Date	Hour	Summary of Events and Information	Remarks and references to Appendices
LE SARS	7/4/18	7am	H.Q. and Nos. 1 & 2 Section moved W.23.a central (Stormlooken Wood) area Harancourt (Sheet 57dE)	JC
Harancourt area	24/4/18	7pm	Column was forced to retire this area by enemy shell fire and moved to location M.22.c.7.8 on the S. by S. East Harancourt Rd.	JC
Harancourt area	24/4/18	6.30 am	No. 2 Section assembled with RHA Brigade and proceeded east to VI Corps area	JC
Harancourt area	24/4/18	9am	No. 1 Section assembled with RHA Brigade & proceeded under orders of the 33rd Div Arty to V.2.b (ELSON COPSE) Sheet 57c	JC
Harancourt area	29/4/18	12 noon	Headquarters only moved to V.21.b (ELSON COPSE) Sheet 57 c	JC
ELSON COPSE	29/4/18	3.30 pm	No. 1 Section moved to W.14.c received orders from 33rd Division	JC

J Cotterell Major
Offg 21st DAC

CONFIDENTIAL.

WAR DIARY

21st Divisional Ammunition Column.

October 1st - 31st - 1918.

Army Form C. 2118.

WAR DIARY
or
INTELLIGENCE SUMMARY.
(Erase heading not required.)

Instructions regarding War Diaries and Intelligence Summaries are contained in F.S. Regs. Part II and the Staff Manual respectively. Title pages will be prepared in manuscript.

Place	Date	Hour	Summary of Events and Information	Remarks and references to Appendices
Ubern bye	Oct 7th	1330	Head Quarters moved to Fermenell. Nos 1 & 2 (578) No 1 + 2 Sections opened from 33rd RA + VII Corps respectively on this date.	NC
Fermenell (578)	1th Oct	1560	Head Quarters No 1 & 2 Sections moved to Camp N33 (378) between VAUCELLES Copse + CAMBRIA – LE CATELET Rd	NC
N33	11th Oct	10 in	Head Quarters + Nos 1 + 2 Sections moved to J31 a 6.5 (57B) alongside CHUDET – BERTRY Rd	NC
J31 a 6.5	27th Oct	15h.	Head Quarters and Nos 1 + 2 Sections moved to camp at sunken crossroads of AMERIAL – On MAREVAL – OVILLERS Rd K4 + 4.3. Column halted at MENNILLY from 17.30h to 20 hrs.	NC
			During above period the column furnished units 17th and 21st Divisions alternately and also G.7 wagons was attached with their respective Brigades.	NC

H. Conick Capt
Aug 26th D.A.C.

2353 Wt. W2344/1454 700,000 5/15 D.D.&L. A.D.S.S./Forms/C. 2118.

CONFIDENTIAL.

WAR DIARY

OF

21st Divisional Ammunition Column R.F.A.

FROM 1st November 1918.   TO   30th November 1918.

WAR DIARY
OR
INTELLIGENCE SUMMARY.
(Erase heading not required.)

Army Form C. 2118.

Instructions regarding War Diaries and Intelligence Summaries are contained in F.S. Regs. Part II. and the Staff Manual respectively. Title pages will be prepared in manuscript.

Place	Date	Hour	Summary of Events and Information	Remarks and references to Appendices
AMERVAL	Nov 3rd 1915	12.00	Column reinforced by 150 Reservists sent for training and in course of replacing 4 horses of Bethel troop.	JC
AMERVAL	Nov 5th	10.30	H.Q's of No. 1 & 2 Sections moved to 796.37 (Sheet 57 D) 2nd encampment of horsemen of Pon au Nord.	JC
PONT DU NORD	Nov 7th	12.30	H.Q. of No. 1 & 2 Sections moved to LOCQUINON, FOREST DE MORMAL, and encamped on Vacquemia - St Quentin Rd.	JC
LOCQUINON	Nov 9th	9.30	H.Q. of No. 1 & 2 Sections moved to AMIENRES encamped at 11.22 H2 of Sheet 57.	JC
AMIENRES	Nov 11th	21.00	Armistice signed came into operation. D.T. wagons reported the Column formed of Bignar.	JC
AMIENRES	Nov 12th	22.15	Lieut Fraser + of No. 1 & 2 Sections moved to MONTAY near LE CATEAU and billets in the villages.	JC

Norbert Scott
Capt RAVC

CONFIDENTIAL.

WAR DIARY

OF

21st Divisional Ammunition Column R.F.A.

FROM:- December 1st.   TO:- December 31st 1918.

Army Form C. 2118.

WAR DIARY
or
INTELLIGENCE SUMMARY.
(Erase heading not required.)

Place	Date	Hour	Summary of Events and Information	Remarks and references to Appendices
MONTAY	11/12/18	16:00	S.A.A Section rejoined the Units and billeted in FOREST.	
MONTAY	12/12/18	09:00	The Column together with D.A.H.Q and T M Bde transport marched to AUBENCHIEL AUX BOIS	
AUBENCHIEL AUX BOIS	13/12/18	07:30	The Column marched to TINCOURT AREA and billeted for the night in/near huts near BUIRE	
BUIRE	14/12/18	08:00	The march was continued to CHUIGNOLLES. Billets in Village	
CHUIGNOLLES	15/12/18	08:15	Continued the march to BOUTILLERIE Billets in village	
BOUTILLERIE	16/12/18	07:30	Marched to ST SAVEUR. HQ, Nos 1 and 2 Sections billeted in ST SAVEUR. S.A.A Section billeted in TIRANCOURT.	

H. Boswell Capt R.F.A.
Adjt 21st T A C.

WAR DIARY
or
INTELLIGENCE SUMMARY.
(Erase heading not required.)

21 D Aux Col
21st D.A.C.

Place	Date	Hour	Summary of Events and Information	Remarks and references to Appendices
ST SAUVEUR	1/1/19		Hqrs. Nos. 1 & 2 Sections continued to be billeted at ST SAUVEUR. S.A.A. Section at TIRANCOURT.	
	31/1/19		Investigation of personal accounts continues.	

Manley R.T.A.
O/C 21st D.A.C.

CONFIDENTIAL

WAR DIARY

OF

21st Divisional Ammunition Column, R. F. A.

FROM:- 1st February 1919.   TO :-   28th February 1919.

Army Form C. 2118.

WAR DIARY
or
INTELLIGENCE SUMMARY.
(Erase heading not required.)

Instructions regarding War Diaries and Intelligence Summaries are contained in F. S. Regs., Part II. and the Staff Manual respectively. Title pages will be prepared in manuscript.

21st Divisional Ammn Column

Place	Date	Hour	Summary of Events and Information	Remarks and references to Appendices
St SAUVEUR	1-2-19 to 5-2-19		Hdqrs, Nos I and II Sections continue to be billeted at St SAUVEUR, Ammn Section at TINCOURT.	A/5
			Demobilization of personnel and animals continues.	A/5

N Hoy. Capt H.C.
Adjutant 21st Divl.

Army Form C. 2118.

Vol 43

WAR DIARY
or
INTELLIGENCE SUMMARY.

(Erase heading not required.)

21st Divl Amm Column

Instructions regarding War Diaries and Intelligence Summaries are contained in F.S. Regs., Part II. and the Staff Manual respectively. Title pages will be prepared in manuscript.

Place	Date	Hour	Summary of Events and Information	Remarks and references to Appendices
St Saulve	1-3-19 to 31-3-19		Nos. I and No II Sections continue to do duties at St Saulve. Sub Section to do TIRANCOURT. Demobilisation of men (45 approx) continues. All Vehicles of the Column were broadcasted at the 21st Division Cadre Park LONGPRÉ.	R.S.L. R.S.L. R.S.L.

N Moy Capt & Actg
Adjutant 21st DAC

2353 Wt. W2511/1454 700,000 5/15 D.D.&L. A.D.S.S./Forms/C.2118.

WAR DIARY
or
INTELLIGENCE SUMMARY.

(Erase heading not required.) 21st Divisional Ammunition Column.

Army Form C. 2118.

Place	Date	Hour	Summary of Events and Information	Remarks and references to Appendices
St Sauveur	4/4/19		NDPs Nos I, II and Sub Sections moved by march route to LONG, Somme.	481 4 4 189
	30/4/19		Continue to be billetted at LONG, awaiting embarkation R.E. for United Kingdom	

N Blore Capt.
Adjutant
21st D.A.C.

www.ingramcontent.com/pod-product-compliance
Lightning Source LLC
Chambersburg PA
CBHW081556160426
43191CB00011B/1949